DON'T DIE IN YOUR WILDERNESS

How to Bounce Back From Life Changing Events

By John Williams

Bounce Back From Life Changing Events

DON'T DIE IN YOUR WILDERNESS
(How to Bounce Back From Life Changing Events)
Copyright © 2013 by John Williams

All rights reserved. No part of this book may be reproduced or transmitted in any form or by any means without written permission from the author.

Photography: "Photo's by Summers" 419.283.4368

Book Cover design by:
"EverlastingDezigns.com" 419.242.3607

Editorial process completed by: LaToya R. Williams, C.E.O, "Pieces of Me Editorial Services"
419.322.0438
pomeditorialfirm@gmail.com

ISBN: 978-0-615-84515-9

Printed in the United States of America

Praise for: "Don't Die in Your Wilderness"

We cannot control the turmoil life sends our way but we can determine how we respond to it. Like John Williams, we will have a morning when it seems as if life is taking out all of its fury on us. We must be like him and "refuse to die" in the wilderness of turmoil. All of us owe Williams our appreciation for sharing his deepest pain so that we can be guided out of our own.

Remember: No matter how bad the situation, we yet have to make the decision about our next step. Even when life wants to cripple us and make us feel worthless because things are outside of our control; we must encourage ourselves. Let's make the best decision even in what appears to be the worst situation. Just like me, you will be a better individual after reading this book.

Bishop Thomas Wesley Weeks Sr.
Presiding Prelate of New Destiny
Fellowship International,
Pastor of New Destiny Fellowship

Bounce Back From Life Changing Events

Dedication

I dedicate this book to my mother, Doris Williams Johnson. You were and remain the epitome of perseverance, stability, dedication and strength. Your example has shaped the lives of many. Your relationship with God has set the stage for your children, grandchildren and generations to come. I know God because of you. I thank you and love you.

Don't Die In Your Wilderness

Table of Contents

Acknowledgements   6

Introduction   8

1. There's Purpose For Your Pain   11

2. The Paradox   23

3. It Won't Work   35

4. Absalom Is Dead   49

5. Do Everything Right   57

6. Ready Or Not   71

7. After This   87

8. Don't Die In Your Wilderness   95

Resources   105

Acknowledgements

I am enormously grateful to my children Zion and Jonathan II. You two have possessed great patience and understanding in the many assignments I have been given. Outside of my relationship with God, the both of you are most important in my life. You two are amazingly gifted. The world awaits the greatness that will be released from your lives. I love you both.

Special thanks to my ten brothers and sisters. You have supported and underguirded me in ways unmentionable. I am forever grateful. Now, if I didn't mention my brother Mark Williams individually, I know I wouldn't hear the last of it. So, thank you for supporting me through the years. Also, to my father, the late James Williams, I will never forget you.

Much love and thanks to the River of Life Church. Your support, understanding and encouragement keep me going. "Everything Lives at the River."

Many special thanks to the Williams and Taylor families.

Don't Die In Your Wilderness

Kevin Lent I am enormously grateful for our friendship.

Dr. Pat McKinstry I literally do not have the words to say to you. Your wisdom, insight and understanding of God are proof that you are His daughter. Thank you for making time for me during my wilderness experience. The many hours of Godly instruction allowed me to see beyond what could have destroyed me. Thank you and may you receive a 100-fold return on all that you have given to the Body of Christ and unto me.

To my editor LaToya Williams (Pieces of Me Editorial Services) your knowledge, expertise and professionalism are second to none. I am elated for the opportunity I had working with you on my first book. Thanks a million!

Bounce Back From Life Changing Events

Introduction

"DON'T DIE IN YOUR WILDERNESS"

(How to Bounce Back From Life Changing Events)

I will never forget the Sunday morning I arose early. I had done this for years, to prepare to minister to the church I pastor. I found out quickly that something was different about this particular morning. I never made it to my office. As I sat in my living room I began to weep uncontrollably. I could not concentrate. I began to experience challenges in my health. A short time after this, the stress of financial difficulties took a toll. This didn't only happen to me but my church as well. As if I wasn't already dealing with enough; out of nowhere my son was wrongfully expelled from the school he had attended for years. Later, my daughter met challenges and then it happened. **The big boom!** The marriage I had invested in for 18 years began to unravel at a pace I could not control. To add insult to injury, my personal matters became very public. The result was slander, lies and malicious attacks.

After three months of extensive prayer and counsel I decided to do what I call "the unthinkable," *I filed for a divorce.* During this horrible, mind boggling process I remember thinking, "this must be a dream. This can't be happening to me! **How did I get here?**" The bottom fell out completely. I was left with thoughts of anger, loneliness and fear at its highest level. I had preached, taught and sung before thousands. I was spreading the good news and encouraging people to move forward. Yet, somehow I was at a standstill and felt like someone had pushed the pause button on my entire life. I know this must sound unfair and it is; but this is **not** the end of my story.

Yes, bad things can happen to good people. As a matter of fact, it was happening to me. Have you ever been tested, tried and stretched far beyond the Richter scale? This is a place of confusion, bewilderment and extreme isolation. This is the place where the thought of giving up and quitting seems to be the only logical answer. I have news for you. **This is only the wilderness experience**. The wilderness is a metaphor for a place of confusion, wanderings and testing. It is also the place of growth and shaping. What's even better than that, it is the place where God will make Himself known.

Join in with me, **release** the pause button and press play. Throughout the rest of the pages in this book, I will share with you some invaluable lessons I learned throughout my journey. It is my prayer that you will see the jewels mixed within the junk. I want you to embrace purpose after pain, learn from every life experience and at least know it's possible that your greatest days are ahead of you. "Don't die in your wilderness, prepare to bounce back!"

Chapter One

THERE IS PURPOSE FOR YOUR PAIN

One thing that people have in common is the fact that all have experienced some form of pain. Whether it was for a long or short period of time; pain has made its acquaintance with every living being. Have you ever wondered what purpose your pain would serve? Why do we experience it and what would life be like without it? I think it would be fair to say, if you're reading this book and don't know me, you are experiencing some form of pain or have already walked through a painful situation. Even if you do know me, I'm certain you've had your share of pain.

One of Webster's definitions of pain is: the distress or suffering, mental or physical, caused by great anxiety, anguish, grief or disappointment. I know we see pain as a negative thing in our lives. When you really think about it, who wants to experience pain? There is a part of pain that can be enormously helpful. Pain is an indicator that something is wrong. Pain is one of the things that we don't like. It can be a discomfort, to say the least. Have you ever taken the wrong turn and you knew you were going the wrong way? Personally, that is one of the worst feelings. Let's just say pain functions similar to a GPS system. A good GPS system will alert you if you're going the wrong way. A toothache can indicate that you may need a filling or root canal. A headache could indicate you are stressed and or may need to check your blood pressure. Likewise, pain will alert you when something is misaligned and needs attention. It is simply an indicator that something is wrong.

While it is the issues of life that brings pain, it is enormously paramount that we acknowledge pain. We must pinpoint the root cause and finally move forward to finding a solution.

Pain Is Part of the Process

One of the most rehearsed stories in the bible is that of Joseph. At the tender age of seventeen he had a dream that he would be in a great place of leadership. This dream depicted that his family would have to look to him for guidance. Joseph was so excited that he shared the dream with his family. Well, it caused him to be envied even the more.

"Now Israel loved Joseph more than all his children, because he was the son of his old age. Also he made him a tunic of many colors.

But when his brothers saw that their father loved him more than all his brothers, they hated him and could not speak peaceably to him.

Now Joseph dreamed a dream, and he told it to his brothers; and they hated him even the more."

Genesis 37:3-5

Joseph found out very quickly that being his father's favorite along with having a call from God came with a price. No doubt, Joseph experienced pain from his brothers. Pain was a part of his process. Many times in walking with the Lord, He will show you the end result but may not always fill you in on the in-betweens (the process). While on his way to fulfilling the dream, Joseph experienced what many refer to as the four P's; the pit, Potiphar's house, the prison and finally the palace.

Joseph's brothers initially wanted to kill him, but decided to sell him into slavery instead. Sometimes the worst pain can come from the hands of those who are trusted family members or close relationships that are supposed to guard, love and support us. Can you imagine Joseph hearing and seeing the plot against him by his own flesh and blood? No doubt, this brought feelings of anger, rejection, turmoil and abandonment.

"So it came to pass, when Joseph had come to his brothers, that they stripped Joseph of his tunic, the tunic of many colors that was on him.

Don't Die In Your Wilderness

Then they took him and cast him into a pit. And the pit was empty; there was no water in it.

So Judah said to his brothers, 'What profit is there if we kill our brother and conceal his blood?

Come let us sell him to the Ishmaelites, and let not our hand be upon him, for he is our brother and our flesh.' And his brothers listened."

Genesis 37:23, 24, 26, 27

After being sold into slavery Joseph landed in Potiphar's house. He was wrongfully accused and sent to prison. Joseph's entire life had taken major turns. We must remember that things happen in life. Unfortunately, bad things can happen but we must stay focused in this journey called life. It is imperative that we understand we are not defined by the circumstances of our lives. We don't have to succumb to all the negatives and fall prey to the "why me syndrome." Pull yourself up by your bootstraps and know that pain is a part of the process.

Several years passed with Joseph serving a jail sentence for something he didn't do. By this time he's thirty years old. No doubt he probably felt that alone. I think it would be fair to say he had to have thought "what happened to the dream?' What's interesting is that thirteen years had passed and it didn't seem like things would ever be the same. All of the events Joseph experienced were a part of his process. If you are going to live life free of worries, anxiety and stress you will have to acknowledge that it's not just about getting to the finish line. Paying close attention to the details and learn to navigate through your process. There are many invaluable lessons the process can teach you, if you will allow yourself to be a student.

Getting Even vs. Getting Better

It is an undeniable fact that many people spend their lives rehearsing all the bad things that happened to them. To be more specific I met countless people who have not figured out that the processes of life are important.

However, the way we respond is significant. In fact, your response to all the situations of life will determine where you will end up. Another undeniable fact is that the prison systems are filled with people who responded the wrong way. Unfortunately there are those that "have to get the last lick." As a child my brothers, sisters and I would indulge in horseplay while enjoying each other's company. We would love playing the game, "getting the last lick." This game was one that simply meant you felt vindicated if you were able to serve the last hit or blow. Just like children right? What's amazing is that I see adults engage in this activity quite frequently.

Many shift their focus and attention to getting even with the one whom they feel wronged them. This is a dangerous place to be in. Getting even can drive a person to do the unthinkable. Getting even can make a person loose sight of the important things in life, while pursuing revenge at any cost. Getting even can take you so far away from your beliefs that it will shock you; this is why we are seeing breakdowns within families. Many have opted out of forgiving, in exchange for tearing down the character of other people. The irony to all of this is that getting even doesn't always fix the problem. When it's all said and done the root of the problem still remains. Getting even does not eradicate scars that are buried deep within.

Getting better is where our focus should be. It is wise to put our energy, focus and resources towards getting better, as opposed to getting even. Getting better assures you of a bright and promising future. Getting better is the right way to handle the wrongs of life. This is what separates the men from the boys. Let's look at an interesting point of revelation with Joseph.

As God would have it, a series of events happened and shifted things in Joseph's favor. Pharaoh had a dream in which no one could interpret, everyone tried but failed. It was during this time that Pharaoh's butler remembered Joseph. He was the man who had interpreted his dream while in prison. Joseph was given the opportunity to go before Pharoah to interpret his troubling dreams. Well of course, after the accuracy of the interpretation, Joseph was elevated to second in command. He was in charge of all that Pharaoh had. Some say he had the position of a governor or in today's view, a Vice President. Joseph was given the authority of distributing the food supply to all the people. Through this elevation he was reunited with his brothers and father. After the father's death, Joseph had the prime opportunity to get even with his brothers.

Let's look at his response:

"When Joseph's brothers saw that their father was dead, they said, 'Perhaps Joseph will hate us, and may actually repay us for all the evil which we did to him.'

So they sent messengers to Joseph, saying, 'Before your father died he commanded, saying, Thus you shall say to Joseph: I beg you, please forgive the trespass of your brothers and their sin; for they did evil to you. Now, please, forgive the trespass of the servants of the God of your father.' And Joseph wept when they spoke to him.

Then his brothers also went and fell down before his face, and they said, 'Behold we are your servants.'

Joseph said to them, 'Do not be afraid, for I am in the place of God?'

But as for you, you meant evil against me; but God meant it for good, in order to bring it about as it is this day, to save many people alive.

Now therefore do not be afraid; I will provide for you and your little ones.' And he comforted them and spoke kindly to them."

Genesis 50:15-21

There are several important factors within this particular subject matter. First and foremost Joseph forgave his brothers. Whenever there is some type of wrong or injustice, forgiveness is the key element to healing and becoming better. You will have to let it go! Forgiving does not mean you weren't harmed in a significant way. It just means you have opted out of getting even to get better. Forgiving is the way to true inward healing.

Secondly, pain is a part of the process. Please notice that as they apologized and spoke to Joseph, he wept. Even after you have forgiven, some pain and trespasses can take enormous amounts of time to heal. But you will get there!

Thirdly there is purpose for your pain. Joseph realized that he was in the place of God. He knew through his dreams, God had planned elevation for his life. He placed more focus on getting to the dream as opposed to what happened along the way. His sole purpose was to save many lives.

Fourthly, he guarded his heart. What I found interesting is at his greatest moment to seek revenge; he comforted his brothers and spoke kindly to them. Even though he suffered at the hands of his brothers, he had reached a place of freedom through forgiveness.

Bounce Back From Life Changing Events

Chapter 2

THE PARADOX

In my introduction I spoke of some of the unfavorable circumstances that I have I faced. Adversity has a way of making its mark in our lives. To be frank, there's another interesting piece to the puzzle. Before my world changed, I had a series of dreams, prophetic words and biblical promises pointing to the fact that I was about to be promoted. With all of this, who wouldn't be excited? I was happy and telling people of great things that were about to happen for me. I began to make preparations and had great hope that things would change at any given time.

I'm sure you can imagine; I was grossly disappointed when my life took a turn for the worst and not for the better. At this point doubt showed up and I began to question if I had really heard right. Was I really a candidate for promotion? Was the dream to be taken literal or did I eat the wrong thing before going to bed? Were the prophecies accurate? Maybe I took the words from the bible out of context! These were my thoughts and feelings due to the fact that what I was witnessing, did not match with what I had seen. This brought on a great deal of confusion until I experienced a powerful revelation.

On the Contrary

An important factor to keep in mind is "things aren't always as they seem." There's a very interesting word that we need to focus on. That word is paradox. According to Webster, a paradox is a statement that seems contradictory, unbelievable or absurd, but may be true. Basically a paradox refers to irony or contradiction. Wow! It all makes sense now. I had received information and even direction from the Lord, but it was in the form of a paradox. It was a truth that presented itself as a contradiction.

After Moses had introduced 10 different plagues upon the Egyptians, they were supposed to let the Israelites go free. That was supposed to be the end.

"And the Lord said to Moses, 'I will bring yet one more plague on Pharoah and on Egypt. Afterward he will let you go from here. When he lets you go, he will surely drive you out of here altogether.'"

Exodus 11:1

On the contrary, this wasn't the end at all. Yes, Pharaoh pushed the Israelites out after the tenth plague, but let's look at what happens after the death of the firstborn:

"Now it was told the King of Egypt that the people had fled, and the heart of Pharoah and his servants was turned against the people; and they said, 'why have we done this that we have let Israel go from serving us?' So he made ready his chariot and took his people with him. Also, he took six hundred choice chariots, and all the chariots of Egypt with captains over every one of them.

And the Lord hardened the heart of Pharoah king of Egypt, and he pursued the children of Israel; and the children of Israel went out with boldness."

Exodus 14:5-8

Notice it was God who said the children of Israel would go free. However, the Egyptians came after Israel one last time. This is the paradox. The truth is Pharaoh did let them go. The contrary comes in when they pursued one last time.

Do you remember the story of Elijah and how he was instructed to drink from the brook Cherith and was fed by ravens?

"Then the word of the Lord came to him, saying, "Get away from here and turn eastward, and hide by the Brook Cherith, which flows into the Jordan. And it will be that you shall drink from the brook, and I have commanded the ravens to feed you there."

I Kings 17:2-4

Notice what happens to the prophet:

"And it happened after a while that the brook dried up, because there had been no rain in the land."

I Kings 17:7

Did you notice what happened? The Lord told him to go to the brook and that he would drink there; however He didn't tell him that it would dry up. The Paradox!

A paradox is a truth that appears contradictory or even false. My best one yet has to do with the patriarch Abram.

"And the Lord said to Abram, after Lot had separated from him: 'Lift your eyes now and look from the place where you are- northward, southward, eastward, and westward; for all the land which you see I give to you and your descendants forever. And I will make your descendants as the dust of the earth; so that if a man could number the dust of the earth, then your descendants also could be numbered.'"

Genesis 13:14-16

Wow! Abram receives a powerful promise that his descendants will be as the number of the dust of the earth. That's a lot of folk! But wait a minute. Abram is 75 years old and has no children. Abram experienced his own personal paradox.

Seeing Is Not Always Believing

I know we've heard the saying, "seeing is believing." Let me assure you that during this journey called life, you will experience seasons where everything you've believed in, worked for and sacrificed will seem contradictory. You may even say; "my whole life has been a paradox." You've got to know that, you don't have to necessarily see something to believe it. Please do not allow your present circumstances to dictate your future blessings, goals and accomplishments. If you're going to embrace the greatness that is destined for your life, you will have to work through contradictions, controversy, problems and challenges. Just because you don't have everything right now, does not mean it won't happen. You may not know where the scholarships are going to come from, but that does not mean you're not going to college. Perhaps you don't have the start up money for your business. That does not mean you will not be an entrepreneur. Maybe you're experiencing uncertainty in a marriage you thought would last (until death do us part). You can have a healthy marriage if the both of you are willing to put in the work.

Believe When You Can't See

Faith is an invaluable asset that we must embrace. Possessing faith and believing will determine how great you will become. Greatness doesn't just show up. Success doesn't accidentally assign itself to a person. Greatness, success, progression, prosperity and even wholeness will come as a result of believing. You must believe first.

To Believe or Not to Believe

Is the glass half empty or half full? How do you view it? We have a choice to believe, remain neutral, or not to believe. You have a choice to believe you will get the job or not. You have a choice to believe you will be healed or not. You have a choice to believe you will find love. Indeed, you must know this; if you don't believe you will get the job then you believe that won't get it. If you don't believe you will be healed then you believe that you won't. If you don't believe you will find love, then you believe that you won't. In each case you believe in the negative as opposed to the positive. Why not believe the positive!

Here are a few practical points I've learned concerning faith:

- Every person is given a measure of faith.
- Faith will be tested in times of uncertainty.
- Faith has to do with action, not just the thought of believing.
- Faith must become a way of life.

- Faith unlocks doors of possibilities.
- Faith is nurtured through hearing God's word.
- Faith is priceless.
- Doubt is the antithesis of faith.

It's your move! It is your time to dry the tears. This is your time to embrace a life of joy, peace and happiness. This is your time to realize there is truth in your personal paradoxes.

A Promise Is a Promise

Be encouraged, God is not like man. He cannot lie. If you have a promise from the Father, GET READY! It doesn't matter how conflicting the situation may appear. If he said it, it will come to pass. I've witnessed people receive prophetic words. I've seen them standing on biblical principles and even having dreams of themselves doing great things; only to have the bottom fall out. Be encouraged! If the promise was from God, you can be sold into slavery but it still won't stop you. You may even experience lies and false accusations.

Just know that if the word is from the Lord, nothing will stop you. If God promised it, you will have it. If God said it, it will come to pass. If it is written, stand on it! He cannot lie! A promise from God is a promise that will be kept, honored and fulfilled.

Turning the Impossible Into Possibilities

Another amazing fact about God is that He has the ability convert our mess into a message. He can turn our junk into jewels. He can turn our impossibilities into possibilities. You may be saying "I didn't plan for my life to end up like this, there's no hope for me now, I'm too old, or I've totally blown every chance at success." Please allow me to challenge your thought process. It's not over and it's not too late! God specializes in unique, difficult, and even challenging cases. It's as if He has the ability to take a person with their back up against the wall, and create a whole new life for them. This is exactly what happened for both Joseph and Abraham. The odds were against both of them. In both cases they were able to soar above their wilderness experiences to great possibilities.

Bounce Back From Life Changing Events

Chapter 3

IT WON'T WORK

You are valuable, you are beautiful and there is purpose for your existence. What I have found interesting is that there are millions upon millions of people who do not believe that statement. Please allow me to prove it through scripture.

"For you have formed my inward parts; you have covered me in my mother's womb. I will praise you, for I am fearfully and wonderfully made; Marvelous are your works, and that my soul knows very well."

Psalm 139:13, 14

Wow! This is proof that you were not an accident. You are not the mistake of your parent's old age. You were fearfully and wonderfully made. God designed your inward parts; each one a testament of His divine craftsmanship.

"Then Moses said to the Lord, O my Lord, I am not eloquent, neither before nor since

you have spoken to your servant; but I am slow of speech and slow of tongue. So the Lord said to him, who has made man's mouth? Or who makes the mute, the deaf, the seeing, or the blind? Have not I, the Lord?"

Exodus 4:10, 11

The Lord teaches an invaluable lesson with His servant Moses. God called Moses to lead the children of Israel. No doubt, he would have to speak. According to Moses, there was one problem. He was slow to speak and possessed speech problems. Ok, you have to know that God has a phenomenal sense of humor. Of all the millions He could've chosen, He chose Moses (the man who could barely talk). Wait, isn't that the miracle of it all? Isn't that the touch of the Divine? Isn't that the favor of God? He created Moses to lead millions of people but yet have a speech problem. God reminds Moses that He is the creator of all human life; that includes the death, blind and mute.

You are unique and special to God and there is purpose for your life. Now that we have established the fact that you are of great value, can't you see why the evil one would want to harm you? I must tell you, "It Won't Work." That's right! "It Won't Work."

There's An Abortionist on the Loose, But It Won't Work

It was during one of my hottest battles that I received phenomenal revelation. I learned that there was a difference between a murderer and an abortionist. A murderer is one who commits the crime of murder. A murderer will target the young, old, male, female, black or white. An abortionist is totally different. Abortion as defined by Webster is any spontaneous expulsion of an embryo or a fetus before it is sufficiently developed to survive. The purpose of an abortionist is to cut off life prematurely in its developing stages. The abortionist wants to terminate a life before it's mature. Let's look in the word of God.

"Then Herod, when he saw that he was deceived by the wise men, was exceedingly

angry; and sent forth and put to death all the male children who were in Bethlehem and in all its districts, from two years old and under, according to the time which he had determined from the wise men."

Matthew 2:16

Notice Herod had every male child under the age of two killed. The nature of this crime was to find and kill the baby Jesus. Herod's purpose was not limited to killing Jesus. He wanted to kill "baby Jesus". His sole plan was to abort the purpose God had assigned to Jesus' life. This is why the strategy attack started when He was a baby. It didn't work! Therefore, it doesn't have to work against you either.

Created For a Specific Purpose

After the fall of man, in the Garden of Eden, God had to intervene so that His creation would not be eternally lost. The Lord, in His providence, set out to reverse the effects of Adam. He loved man so intensely that He did the unthinkable. He gave His only begotten

Son to complete the job. Jesus had a specific purpose in the earth:

- <u>**To save man from eternal damnation.**</u>

    - *Ephesians 2:8, 9 "For by grace you have been saved through faith, and that not of yourselves, it is the gift of God, not of works, lest anyone should boast. For we are His workmanship, created in Christ Jesus for good works, which God prepared beforehand that we should walk in them."*

- <u>**To become the perfect sacrifice.**</u>

    - *Hebrews 2:17 "Therefore, in all things He had to be made like His brethren, that He might be a merciful and faithful High Priest in things pertaining to God, to make propitiation for the sins of the people."*

- <u>**To reconcile man back to Himself.**</u>

    - *Colossians 19, 20 "For it pleased the Father that in*

> *Him all the fullness should dwell, and by Him to reconcile all things to Himself, by Him, whether things on earth or things in heaven, having made peace through the blood of His cross."*

It is evident and clear that Jesus had a purpose and was on assignment in the earth. Did you notice it was the spirit of the abortionist that tried to prematurely annihilate His purpose? The evil one wasn't just interested in killing Jesus. He wanted to prevent the death, burial and resurrection of our Lord and Savior.

Guard Your Purpose

Meet George, he's a Christian man of integrity. He also possesses impeccable morals. George and his siblings were raised by their mother in an environment of great lack. Although George was highly intelligent, his low self-esteem seemed to remind him of his meager upbringing. George had planned to be the first one in his family to go to college until his science teacher reinforced what he had heard all his life. "You are not college material. Why don't you just get a job and be happy you can at least work." Unfortunately, George succumbed to the pressures of his teacher and surroundings and gave up on college. Wow! Can it really happen that easily? Yes it can! George could've completed his education and opened his computer business. To be frank, it was nothing more than the spirit of the abortionist. All along he was strategizing to kill the dreams, goals and visions within George. Let me remind you that the abortionist will go after that which is premature. The abortionist will also seek what has not materialized.

Use the Power Within

Could it be that your marriage can work? Is it possible that you can be the artist that you were destined to be? Do you believe you can obtain your PhD? Could it be that you can own your own business and employ people? The only one stopping you is "the man in the mirror." Once you have identified the works of the abortionist, it is time to use the power within. It is time to feed your faith and starve your doubts. You have the master plan! You have the blueprint! What are you waiting on? You must join me in releasing the pause button and pushing play. It is your time and your turn. Every person was created with a measure of faith. In other words, you have everything you need to succeed.

How to Opt Out of the Failure Plan

Meet Susan, a woman who was acquainted with grief in ways unimaginable. Susan was from the "All American" family. On the outside it looked like her family had everything; the perfect mother, devoted father, 2 dogs and a house with a picket fence. Everyone wanted to pattern after this family, they just had all it together. What people didn't know was that Susan's mother was addicted to pain medication and would leave the family for days at a time. To make matters worst, Susan's mother would steal all the money designated to pay the utilities. If that wasn't enough she was known to have a couple of outside flings with younger men. Unfortunately the mother's lifestyle destroyed the family. Susan was left feeling hurt, disappointed and resentful towards her mother. Susan decided that she would not react negatively to her mother's wrongdoings. She finished school, married her college sweetheart and became a pharmacist. Ten years into the marriage Susan's husband, Dan was diagnosed with a rare disease that caused enormous financial strains and problems within the home. One day when Susan thought she was at her wits end, the thought came to just take a few pills to promote relaxation. In an effort to cope with the daily stresses, Susan began befriending her relaxation pills. After a few weeks of this Susan heard a message at her church; "There's An Abortionist on the Loose, but It Won't Work." Susan quickly sought help from her pastor and doctors and was able to stop the family cycle that was presented. The truth of the matter is, it was the spirit of the abortionist. The attempt was to kill her dreams, destroy her marriage of 10 years and prematurely destroy the lives of all those around her. It had always been Susan's dream to remain married. She'd planned to be a successful pharmacist and a model that women could pattern themselves after. I'm so pleased to tell you, she did just that! Susan opted out of agreeing with the tactics of the abortionist and embraced all of her dreams. She decided that she would not allow destructive behaviors to kill her goals, dreams and aspirations prematurely.

On the Winning Team

There was always something about going to a ball game and sitting on the side of those who had a reputation for winning. There's a certain feeling one experience when they walk in the gym and take a seat on the side of the winning team. On this side you can smell victory. On this side you will speak of your opponents defeat before the game even start. On this side everyone is promoting school pride.

Don't Die In Your Wilderness

Why? It's because they're on the winning team.

That is exactly where you are. You are on the winning team. We must not confuse challenges with that which is seasonal. We must not confuse tragedy with defeat. We must not confuse a season with eternity. Challenges will come, tragedy may present itself and some seasons can be horrific; but you are on the winning team.

"We are hard pressed on every side, yet not crushed; we are perplexed, but not in despair; persecuted, but not forsaken; struck down, but not destroyed."

II Corinthians 4:8, 9

"Many are the afflictions of the righteous, but the Lord delivers him out of them all."

Psalm 34:19

Important keys to remember:

    a) You are not crushed.
    b) You are not in despair.
    c) You are not forsaken.
    d) You are not destroyed.

e) You are delivered out of all your afflictions.

Can't you see these truths? You may be walking through your wilderness but you will come out strong. You may have even experienced attack on every hand, but in the end you will win.

You Are Not Home Alone (There's A Bigger Picture)

One of the greatest things to know in this lifetime is we have help. We don't have to try to figure it out all by ourselves. I've already shared with you about sitting on the side of the winning team. Have you ever been on the side of the team that has the star player? When the champion comes to the court the stadiums will erupt with applause and cheer. When the champion shows up, the confidence level of the winning side rises while fear is evoked in the hearts of the opponents. This is how you should feel about Jesus (the champion of champions). Jesus is your help. He will never leave you. You may be tested but He is ever present. You may even have to deal with the spirit of the abortionist, but you have all the tools to defeat every enemy that present itself.

You are not home alone. There's a bigger picture. Your tests are an indication that greater things are coming and ahead. You must believe in your God-given dreams. The God-given prophecies will come true. There is enormous potential hidden deep within you. Don't forget that you are fearfully and wonderfully made. Your tests and struggles are only a means to strengthen your muscles of faith. God allowed your tests to bring the best out of you. It's time to wipe the tears from your eyes and make conscious decisions to defeat the spirit of the abortionist. It's time to move on with life. After all, you have Jesus (the champion of champions) on your team.

"Fear not, for I am with you; be not dismayed, for I am your God. I will strengthen you, Yes, I will help you, I will uphold you with my righteous right hand."

Isaiah 41:10

Bounce Back From Life Changing Events

Chapter 4

ABSALOM IS DEAD
(*Let Go and Move On*)

You're probably wondering what this chapter is about and who is Absalom? I'm so glad you asked. In II Samuel chapters 13 through 18 there's a very unique and interesting story of King David and his beloved son Absalom. The story of King David and Absalom includes murder, betrayal, lies and heartbreak. Absalom killed his brother Amnon for raping their sister, Tamar. Absalom waited for two years and then made his move. After his brothers' death, he fled for his life. After being away he was received back and then began dividing his father's kingdom while building his own. This took years and a crafty, cunning heart. Basically, Absalom and his followers created their own kingdom. Please be aware of a biblical truth that cannot be denied. If God doesn't call a thing, it will not prosper. Even though Absalom created his own kingdom, the anointing rested upon David. Let's look at how both David and Absalom came into office:

"So he sent and brought him in. Now he was ruddy, with bright eyes, and good looking. And the Lord said, Arise, anoint him; for this is the one! Then Samuel took the horn of oil and anointed him in the midst of his brothers; and the Spirit of the Lord came upon David from that day forward. So Samuel arose and went to Ramah."

I Samuel 16:12, 13

"But Absalom, whom we anointed over us, has died in battle."

II Samuel 19:10

It is very clear that David was God's choice and selection. Absalom was the people's choice. It is always wise to embrace the plan of the Lord as opposed to what looks good. God will pay for what He orders. When we allow ourselves to be driven by our flesh, we must be prepared to pay the cost.

When it's Dead, It's Dead!

As a pastor I have ministered to countless people for situations I thought were current issues. I did this only to find that they were past issues. Please understand I am not dismissing the fact that traumatizing situations can have long lasting affects on people. Also, I am not just saying "get over it." What I am saying, is we have a choice to accept the dead things in our lives. We must understand that they can hold us back and eventually rob us of our freedom, joy and peace. What I find interesting is that David was mourning the death of a son who had been trying to kill him. Absalom and his men were defeated. David's sorrow and grief was so strong that it turned their victory into defeat.

"And Joab was told, Behold, the king is weeping and mourning for Absalom. So the victory that day was turned into mourning for all the people. For the people heard it said that day; the king is grieved for his son."
II Samuel 19:1, 2

Bounce Back From Life Changing Events

The people were astonished at the fact that this great king who possessed great victories with a lion, a bear and Goliath was on the run. It was a known fact that God was with David. Yet, the people had a very valid point. "Why is David out of his position when Absalom is dead?"

"Now all the people were in a dispute throughout all the tribes of Israel, saying, The king saved us from the hand of our enemies, he delivered us from the hand of the Philistines, and now he has fled from the land because of Absalom. But Absalom, whom we anointed over us, has died in battle."

II Samuel 19:9,10a

When one does not remove themselves from that which is dead, it can stop their progress. In fact, it can cause them to be out of position. Isn't this the case with David? He should've been in Jerusalem running the kingdom, but instead he was at the gate grieving a son that died trying to kill him.

When something is dead, we are not to allow it to rule or reign in our lives.

Many people are controlled by dead things. I am specifically speaking of past (dead) issues. Some have lost jobs, houses and their financial security due to a failing economy. A job does not define you! You can get another job. A house does not define you. You can rebuild your credit and buy again. Unfortunately many are still crying over dead things as opposed to updating their résumé's and starting over. When something dies in your life, it is time to devise a plan for the next leg of the journey. Your life is not over.

Let It Go

There are times within life's journey when we will have to let go. Let go of whatever is hindering us from making progress. It cannot control you any longer. It is over. You are not a crying, helpless kid anymore. You survived! The dead relationships that had you on a destructive path are over. This is your day of victory. Can't you see it? You have the power now. You have all the tools to live a successful life. You have to let the dead remain dead, and let it go.

You must:

a) Let go of past hurts.
b) Let go of evil words spoken over you.
c) Let go of the thought of getting revenge.
d) Let go of playing the victim for the rest of your life.
e) Let go of; "those were the good ole days."
f) Let go of; "it wasn't supposed to be this way."
g) Let go of whatever's hindering your process.
h) Let go of "I wish I would've, could've and should've."

Move On

One of the greatest ways to "move on," (especially after a life change) is to try new things.

Don't Die In Your Wilderness

Here are a few suggestions:

- Start a new diet to become health conscious.
- Join a gym or fitness club.
- Build your relationship with God: attend church, become a student of God's word and enhance your prayer time.
- Plan a trip.
- Read a good book.
- Sign up for a cooking class.
- Spend more time with those close to you.

Life is what you make of it my friend. God has entrusted you with one of the most precious, valuables ever; and that is life. Enjoy each and every day. Make the decision that you will move on and began to live and not just exist.

I cannot stress enough the importance of moving on. This is exactly why many people die in their wilderness experiences. An inability to move on causes one to become immobile, paralyzed and unproductive.

Live Life to the Fullest

"The thief does not come except to steal, and to kill and to destroy. I have come that they may have life, and that they may have it more abundantly."

John 10:10

Chapter 5

DO EVERYTHING RIGHT

As we continue on this great journey, let me remind you that every person will experience life changes, which will prompt a reaction. I don't need to remind you that both good and evil exist in our world. Being human, makes it fair to say that their will be times when we will be tempted to do what is pleasing to us. Although, what seems pleasing compared to what is right can be totally different. It is at these times that one will quickly find out what they're made of.

It happened during the darkest days of my life when I was presented with some serious choices. I was in the middle of the fire. I was being tested far beyond what I had ever imagined. I was in my own personal wilderness. I felt alone, disappointed and misused. I was facing both, lies and slander that had the propensity to destroy everything I had worked for. It was at this point that I decided that I was fed up with handling things "the Christian way." It was now time to "fight fire with fire." It was about 5:30 a.m. on a Sunday morning and my mind was racing. "I'm not going out like this, I won't allow people to hurt me any longer and I haven't been saved all my life," were just a few of my thoughts. I would like to tell you that I was up praying before service. However, that would be far from the truth. Right in the middle of my many negative thoughts my phone began to ring. It was my father in the gospel, Bishop Thomas Weeks, Sr. I began to tell him of all the horrible things spoken against me and done towards me. I knew without a doubt that he wanted the best for me and would tell me the truth. After my rambling and complaining, he said one phrase, "you must do everything right." I wanted to ask him, "Did you hear me? Do you hear the pain in my voice? Have you taken in consideration all that I've lost?" Yes my friend, he heard me correctly. Consequently, he gave me a very practical but extremely profound instruction. "Do everything right!" is what he said to me again. I must admit, this was not the answer I was expecting. I didn't understand what implications and results "doing everything right" would have. Oh, but I was soon to find out this invaluable lesson.

Doing Right Keeps God on Your Side

I cannot express how important it is to be in right standing with God. It makes all the difference in the world. When we make the decision to do things God's way, it keeps Him on our side. Wow! Do you realize how powerful that statement is? When we do things His way, we become His responsibility.

"Blessed are those who are persecuted for righteousness' sake, for theirs is the kingdom of heaven. Blessed are you when they revile and persecute you, and say all kinds of evil against you falsely for My sake. Rejoice and be exceedingly glad, for great is your reward in heaven, for so they

persecuted the prophets who were before you."

Matthew 5:10-12

"For You, O Lord, will bless the righteous; with favor. You will surround him as with a shield."

Psalm 5:12

"God shall judge the righteous and the wicked, for there shall be a time there for every purpose and for every work."

Ecclesiastes 3:17b

The Truth, the Whole Truth and Nothing but the Truth

As I continued my conversation with my father in the gospel, Bishop Thomas Weeks, Sr., he gave me another invaluable lesson. He said to me "the truth will be the truth for a hundred years (basically forever), but a lie will not be able to stand nor survive." As I began to study this subject, I found out God had a lot to say concerning it.

Sometimes we are concerned when people lie on us. I found out that it does more harm to them than it does the on being lied on. Let's look to the scripture:

"And you shall know the truth, and the truth shall make you free. They answered Him, we are Abraham's descendants, and have never been in bondage to anyone. How can you say, you will be made free? Jesus answered them, most assuredly, I say to you; whoever commits sin is a slave of sin."

John 8:32-34

Wow, Jesus taught a powerful lesson. "You shall know the truth and the truth shall make you free." It is clearly seen here that the truth frees us. I'm going to ask you a question. What is the opposite of a truth? You answered correctly, a lie. If the truth frees us, then it is clear that a lie causes us to be in bondage. In actuality when a person speaks lies, it causes them to be a slave to that certain sin. When a person engages in lying, they will soon find out it will take on a life of itself. Lying will release guilt, shame, and self-imprisonment. You don't have to try to defend yourself. Truth will stand up and call out your name. No matter how things may look, the truth is always the best option.

Modus Operandi

Modus Operandi is a Latin phrase, translated as a "method of operation." This term is used to describe someone's habits or manner of working. It is used particularly in the context of business or criminal investigations. A person's MO has to do with the manner in which they do things or conduct themselves. At all cost, one must remain true to who they are, and not react negatively causing them to step out of character. Some of our life changes are the direct results of bad choices other people have made. It is at these times we must hold true to our MO. We must not allow our reactions to take us far away from what is right.

Your Modus Operandi is to do what is right. Even if others deviate from this truth, remain faithful to what is right. It will bring great rewards in the end.

Meet Alice, a well-respected Certified Public Accountant. Alice started her career from a very humbling beginning, working her way to partnership. Through other colleagues, Alice heard about some new practices that would benefit the company but short-change her clients. These practices were dishonest in nature. Alice was known to cross every "T" and dot every "I". There wasn't a dishonest bone in her body. These new practices were not her MO. Even though she was tempted to make lots of money for the company, she didn't. Instead, Alice decided to remain true to herself, keep her integrity and "do everything right." Alice totally dismissed the new methods and remained predictable in the way she conducted business.

Sowing and Reaping

Any good farmer will tell you there are certain principles that work in farming. First and foremost, you must have a clear understanding of sowing and reaping. Whatever you sow you will reap. This is paramount in your discussion of "Doing Everything Right." A good farmer knows that if he/she wants to grow tomatoes, he/she must plant tomato seeds. You can't plant cucumber seeds and look for tomatoes. Reaping what you sow is a spiritual law as well. If you want good to come to you, you must sow good seed. The same principle applies for the negative. This is exactly why you cannot afford to react negatively. The laws of sowing and reaping are in full affect.

"While the earth remains, seedtime and harvest, and cold and heat, and winter and summer, and day and night shall not cease."

Genesis 8:22

As long as the earth remains there will be summer and winter, day and night, cold and heat. Now if we can see it in action in that statement, we should be able to believe that it will happen with our seed as well. Our actions are seeds. Whatever we sow, we must expect the principle to work and yield its fruit.

Let's look at it another way. When we do good (sowing good seeds) we are storing away good things for our future. It is imperative that you safeguard your future by doing well. Greatness calls for one to be able to ignore the evils that will show up on a daily basis.

Touched By an Angel

One of the premiere blessings in life is to be surrounded by strong, courageous people of faith who will lead you in the right direction at any cost. I must tell you, God shined on my life in more than one way. I have been given the gift of family and friends. I call them angels! I've already spoke of my father in the gospel. Let me add two more instrumental gifts to the equation:

Mother Doris Johnson (my mother) and Dr. Pat McKinstry. During my wilderness period, these three key people in my life gave me truth on a regular basis. Even though they were seeing me at my lowest point of life, they never told me what I wanted to hear. They told me what was right; this is enormously paramount. A true friend or family member will not buy into your misery, in an attempt to give you a quick fix.

It has always been my philosophy to have a small circle of well-trusted, tried and true people in my corner. These people will genuinely lead me down the correct paths in life. There are times when our pain, circumstances and personal wilderness experiences can block our view as to what is right. These are the times when you call on your angels. A best friend or relative who will tell you what you want to hear, as opposed to truth is not your angel. These are not people you should receive advice from. Wrong advice is wrong advice, even if it comes from a parent, brother, sister, etc. Shall I remind you that your actions today are seeds that will grow tomorrow? Angels will give you wisdom, which will perfectly align you for greatness.

"Hear, my son, and receive my sayings, and the years of your life will be many. I have taught you in the way of wisdom; I have led you in right paths. When you walk, your steps will not be hindered, and when you run, you will not stumble. Take firm hold on instruction, do not let go; Keep her, for she is your life."

Proverbs 4:10-13

Give Yourself the Gift of Forgiveness

One of the greatest gifts you can give yourself is forgiveness. When you forgive it will ultimately be an enormous blessing for you. We are commanded by God to forgive so that our own sins would be forgiven. W. E. Vines define forgiveness as: to let loose from or to release. When we forgive we are following God's instructions by releasing our offenders. To forgive is to loose our offenders from the offence. In return we free ourselves. Forgiveness doesn't mean the offender didn't commit the offence. Forgiveness is to let go of resentment and any thought of revenge. Forgiveness doesn't mean we deny the responsibility of our offenders. It means you will make the conscious decision to free yourself and those who have caused you pain.

Here are a few lessons that can aide in your forgiveness process:

- Forgiveness promotes inner peace.
- Forgiveness can lower blood pressure.
- Forgiveness can combat depression.
- Forgiveness can relieve you from bitterness.

"The weak can never forgive. Forgiveness is the attribute of the strong."

~Mahatma Gandhi~

"Forgiveness is the fragrance that the violet shed on the heel that has crushed it."

~Mark Twain~

Don't Die In Your Wilderness

"Always forgive your enemies; nothing annoys them so much."

~Oscar Wilde~

Bounce Back From Life Changing Events

Chapter 6

READY OR NOT

"Ready or not, here I come." Those were the days! Oh, how I remember playing that game with my friends. One person would close their eyes and count, while the others hid in their secret places. Then it was time to find those that were hiding. Before you started your search, there were those famous words, "ready or not, hear I come!" Even if you didn't have enough time to hide, the person counting would not wait. That is the story of "Life Changing Events." These events will sneak up on you like a predator. Whether you are prepared or unprepared, life happens. It will manifest in changes. What I find interesting is that this is not a new subject. In fact it's an old subject. Based upon a plethora of reasons, people don't always voluntarily welcome change.

Nothing Stays the Same

Winter, summer, spring and fall, nighttime and daytime, grade school, middle school, high school and college, childhood, adolescence, or even adulthood; These are all forms and stages of change that will take place in one's life.

It was a beautiful day and I was extremely nervous due to the fact, it was the first day of school. As we pressed through the crowd, I kept reminding myself that everything was going to work out. She was going to do just fine. The teacher, staff and students would love her. Even though I was nervous, I noticed many of the older kids running, laughing and excited about this day. As we entered the school, I braced myself for what I thought was the inevitable. I had prepared myself for my daughter to weep uncontrollably. After all, she was at a new school, with different kids, and in a new environment. To my surprise, after we walked into the classroom, she greeted her teacher, released my hand, found her assigned seat and waited for class to start. To add insult to injury, she gave me a look as if she wanted to say, "Dad, please leave!" It was a lesson well learned. My daughter was ready and prepared for kindergarten. It was good ole dad who had to adjust to the "new" normal.

Adapt to Change

The thought of making changes can be challenging. When you factor in the wilderness experience, the dynamics are totally different. Don't forget, life changing events will happen regardless. This was the unique situation of the children of Israel. Even though they had been enslaved for over 400 years, they had grown accustomed to their lifestyles.

"And they journeyed from Elim, and all the congregation of the children of Israel came to the Wilderness of Sin, which is between Elim and Sinai, on the fifteenth day of the second month after they departed from the land of Egypt. Then the whole congregation of the children of Israel murmured against Moses and Aaron in the wilderness. And the children of Israel said

to them, Oh, that we had died by the hand of the Lord in the land of Egypt, when we sat by the pots of meat and when we ate bread to the full; for you have brought us out into wilderness to kill this whole assembly with hunger."

Exodus 16:1-3

Did you notice their words ("Oh that we had died by the hand of the Lord in the land of Egypt")? In other words, their brief encounter in the wilderness, mixed with life changes caused them to wish they had died as slaves. They totally dismissed the fact that they had just witnessed signs, wonders and miracles from God. The Lord, in His providence had spared them and their families from all 10 plagues. Being freed from 400 years of bondage was a miracle within itself. Their inability to adapt to change forced them to murmur, complain and wish for what was behind them.

Wow, even though this story took place several thousand years ago, I often witness this same mentality on a regular basis. As we look a little closer, would it be fair to say, they were fearful of what they couldn't control? They knew where their meals were coming from. They knew where they would lay their heads. They had grown accustomed to their lives. I know it's easier said than done. Although change can be difficult, we must learn to adapt to change.

New Growth

Another important lesson is; change can promote growth. As we take a closer look at the children of Israel and their walk with the Lord, it can be said that these changes were opportunities for them to grow. For years they had depended on the Egyptians for food, clothing, water and shelter. This massive change was an opportunity to trust God and possess their own. The life changes that they experienced moved them from a place of slavery to freedom. It moved them from poverty, lack and scarcity to possibilities of prosperity wellness and ownership. They went from idol worship to expanding their relationships with the true, living and Almighty God.

Change can be an opportunity to grow! Perhaps you've rented far too long. Now it's time to own. Maybe you've worked for other companies long enough. Perhaps it's time to start your business. It has been said that "when one door closes, another will open." Embrace this time of change my friend. If you look close enough, you will see there are limitless opportunities ahead of you. In fact, your best days are ahead of you, not behind you."

Allow Yourself Time to Change

Meet David, a well-respected dentist. David had an awesome life. He had a successful practice and was married with three beautiful children. David was a devout Christian. In fact, he would not start his day without spending at least an hour in prayer, bible study and devotion to the Lord. He was convinced that his daily success was predicated upon him giving God the first hour of the day. All went well until David began to notice "trouble in paradise." To his surprise, David's marriage crumbled, leaving him in shock and heartbroken. The devastation of the divorce stole his sleep and appetite. It was normal for David to be up most of the night pondering on what his life would be like. By the time he would fall asleep, the birds would be chirping. These new changes in David's life totally altered his daily routine. As time progressed, the physical and psychologically changes he experienced took a toll. It was clear; he could no longer start his day as he had done for many years. This new change troubled David. In an effort to move forward he scheduled an appointment with his pastor. David's pastor congratulated him on committing himself to the Lord for the first hour of the day. He also encouraged him to adapt to a new time until he could keep his commitment. David welcomed the advice of his pastor and set a new time in the evenings. After several years David was able to return to his morning devotions and learned the valuable lesson of allowing adequate time after a major life change.

Bounce Back From Life Changing Events

Don't Be Afraid, Trust God!

Your wilderness may have totally robbed you of the life you planned. Maybe you don't see how things will ever work out. Perhaps you are silently suffering because someone you depended on dropped the ball. In times of challenge we become fearful. After welcoming fear as a long-lost relative, we feel so alone that we wonder if people even realize we are struggling. I've got good news. Don't be afraid; trust God.

Please consider the following:

    a) *"Call to Me, and I will answer you, and show you great and mighty things, which you do not know."*

                                      Jeremiah 33:3

    b) *"Have I not commanded you? Be strong and of good courage; do not be afraid, nor be dismayed, for the Lord your God is with you wherever you go."*

                                           Joshua 1:9

c) *"When you pass through the waters, I will be with you; and through the rivers, they shall not overflow you. When you walk through the fire, you shall not be burned, nor shall the flame scorch you."*

Isaiah 43:2

d) *"Trust in the Lord, and do good; dwell in the land, and feed on His faithfulness. Delight yourself also in the Lord, and He shall give you the desires of your heart. Commit your way to the Lord, trust also in Him, and He shall bring it to pass."*

Psalm 37:3-5

e) *"I will instruct you and teach you in the way you should go; I will guide you with my eye."*

Psalm 32:8

Govern Your Thoughts

One of the most important factors in life is the ability to think and reason. The mind is one of the most fascinating members of the body. Within the mind one has the ability to think. There has been a lot of dialogue on this subject. It appears as though many people have underestimated the power of their thoughts. One of the greatest scriptures in the bible has to be Proverbs 23:7.

"For as he thinks in his heart, so is he."

Proverbs 23:7

That is a powerful statement! What a phenomenal revelation! "As a man thinks, so is he." Our thoughts will grow, materialize and ultimately bring forth results. No doubt, our thoughts have a lot to do with where we are presently, and where we will be futuristically. I've already spoken about sowing and reaping. I'd like to say that our thoughts are seeds. As I stated before, whatever we sow, we will reap. If this saying is true (and I undoubtedly believe that it is); we have the power to use our thoughts in our process of change. Nothing will change for the good, until your thoughts change for the good.

To Change Your Direction, Change Your Thoughts

We've already established two powerful truths: 1.) Nothing remains the same (change is inevitable). 2.) "As a man thinks, so is he." What if we were to utilize our ability to think, to aide in the entire process of change? If change is going to happen, shouldn't it be for our betterment? This means we must consciously govern our thoughts. You can begin to think about where you need to be. If you think about it long enough, you will find yourself making plans to materialize your thoughts. Just the same, let me remind you of the power of changing your thoughts or "casting down imaginations." You don't have to succumb to negative thoughts. There is power and gifts within you. You are "fearfully and wonderfully made." You are God's investment.

Let's consider a few points from within this lesson:

- Seeing and hearing effects thoughts.
- Actions are the results of thoughts.

- Dismiss negative thoughts, while embracing positive thoughts.
- The character and thoughts of a man are closely related.
- Actions start with a thought.

Gaining a Renewed Mind

I'm amazed at how conscious people are of keeping clean, disinfecting and sanitizing. With all the many germs going around, it is easy to be exposed to sickness and disease. Considering this fact, it is common for someone to pull out hand sanitizer at a restaurant. In fact, it is common for several people at one table to pull out their own personal hand sanitizer. Even at the grocery stores, there are stations available to disinfect the carts before use. Please know I am in full agreement and generally use all of these as preventative measures. Wait a moment! What about the mind? Why aren't we spending quality time cleansing the mind?

"And do not be conformed to this world, but be transformed by the renewing of your

mind, that you may prove what is that good and acceptable and perfect will of God."

Romans 12:2

This has always been one of my favorite scriptures. I both learned and memorized it 16 years ago. It still has the same effect on me when I read it. The world is filled with much evil, wrong and disobedience towards God's will. To be conformed to the world is to become like it. Yes, we live in a world that is influenced by the evil one. Yet, we don't have to conform to its ways and tactics. We are to be transformed. How are we to do all of this with all of the temptations of our day? We are transformed by the renewing of our mind.

Vines describe renewal as "the adjustment of the moral, spiritual vision and thinking to the mind of God, which is designed to have a transforming effect upon the life." It is clear that the mind must be adjusted to Christ-like thoughts. The mind never receives salvation because it is unsaved! This is why we are commanded to "cast down imaginations and every high thing that exalts itself against the knowledge of God (*2 Corinthians 10:5*)." Wow! If the body will follow the mind (thoughts), what would happen if we thought of clean, pure, holy and righteous thoughts? You got it! The body would have to follow. Adjusting your thoughts is a conscious decision. It is not something you will just stumble upon. This is why meditating on the word of God can yield phenomenal results. We must invite the Holy Spirit to govern and cleanse our thought process daily.

Do you see my friend? Transformation (change) occurs after we renew the mind.

Here are a few life keys that will aide in your transformation process:

- Daily prayer concerning your thoughts.
- Reading the word of God regularly.
- Studying the word of God regularly.
- Reading other books of a positive nature (be selective).
- Meditating on scriptures.
- Fasting

- Saying the right things.

Bounce Back From Life Changing Events

Chapter 7

AFTER THIS

"Then He said to Abram: "Know certainly that your descendants will be strangers in a land that is not theirs, and will serve them, and they will afflict them, four hundred years. And also the nation whom they serve I will judge; afterward they shall come out with great possessions."

Genesis 15:13, 14

One of the things I love about God is that He knows how to make the wrongs right in our lives. He has a phenomenal make up plan. He's definitely a God of recompense rewards. Whenever God allow a person to be tested beyond measure, you can rest assure He has already signed their name to the "extreme blessings list." In no way am I advocating that life is all about material things and what we can receive from God. He said it, not me! It is just the way He operates. Let's look a little deeper into *Genesis 15:13, 14*.

Bounce Back From Life Changing Events

He outlines several important key factors:

I. "Your descendants will be strangers in a land that is not theirs."
    a. Without a doubt this is the wilderness experience.

II. "And will serve them."
    a. They would live lives of bondage and slavery.

III. "They will afflict them, four hundred years."
    a. There is purpose for pain!

IV. "And also, the nation whom they serve I will judge."
    a. Sowing and reaping! Don't take matters into your own hands. "Whatever a man sows, he will reap."

V. "Afterward they shall come out with great possession."
    a. When God is in it, He will pay you for all the troubles you've walked through.

Notice how the Lord outlines the wilderness experience, but includes these keys words: "afterward they shall come out with great possessions."

> ***"But may the God of all grace, who called us to His eternal glory by Christ Jesus, after you have suffered a while, perfect, establish, strengthen, and settle you."***
>
> *I Peter 5:10*

Notice in I Peter, the Lord makes it clear that we will walk through periods of suffering. So, if you don't die in your wilderness; He promises to perfect, establish, strengthen and settle you. In other words, you'll have a "bounce back experience!"

Resurrection, Restoration and Completeness (333)

I've already explained how I had dreams, prophetic words and scriptures to confirm that I was in line for promotion. Shortly after the wilderness was unleashed into my life, I noticed something that I thought was strange. One morning I was awakened out of my sleep and noticed it was 3:33 a.m. Not a problem, right? The next day it happened again. I was awakened at exactly 3:33 a.m. The day after that, I was driving and noticed the license plate in front of me. You got it! It read 333. Not long after, I was assigned an account number for some very important matters. I found the number to be 333. This persisted for well over a year. Everywhere I would go there was the number 333. I began researching this in the bible as well as in my prophetic dictionaries. Please be advised, I am not an advocate for weird practices with numbers, colors, etc. It is very clear throughout scriptures that the Lord uses numbers in His system of doing things. For example the number 5 represents *grace*, 7 represents *completeness* and 3 represents *resurrection, restoration,* and *completeness*.

What a mighty God we serve! From the very beginning, the Lord wanted me to know that He would restore all my losses, resurrect everything that died. I knew that God would complete me as a man and make me whole. I have great news. He can do the same for you! Our God is not sitting in heaven waiting on us to make mistakes so that He can condemn us. God loves you sir! God loves you ma'am! Your greatest days are ahead of you, not behind you. If you've walked through any horrible experience, please give it to God and let him handle all your cares. Don't worry about how awful it is. Don't worry about how shameful things look. God is in control and He stands waiting to bless His children.

Restored For the Glory

According to Webster, the word restore means to give back (something taken away or lost); to make restitution; To bring back into being; to bring back to a normal condition by repairing, rebuilding and altering. Not only will the Lord restore you, He will make you better than He did the first time. The next phase of your life can be so great, until you'll think that you're dreaming. Allow the Lord to repair all the damages and restore you for His glory. Move past the tearing down phase, and welcome the divine engineering of our great God. Let Him restore you! Let Him resurrect you! Let Him make you whole and complete as only He can!

Can I Get A Witness?

Within every great court case there is always a witness. The witness is supposed to give an accurate account of what they know. They must answer all questions to the best of their knowledge. The testimony of a witness is considered evidence and carries the same weight as physical objects. The testimony of a witness is not restricted to an oral testimony. A credible witness can make his/her presentation as a written testimony as well. To accurately present my case, please allow me to read the testimonies of my witnesses. The court now calls for the testimonies of Joseph, Job and Ruth.

The Testimony of Joseph

"Then his brothers also went and fell down before his face, and they said, 'behold we are your servants.' Joseph said to them; 'do not be afraid, for am I in the place of God? But as for you, you meant evil against me; but God meant it for good, in order to bring it about as it is this day, to save many people alive.

Now therefore, do not be afraid; I will provide for you and your little ones.' And he comforted them and spoke kindly to them."

Genesis 50:18-21

The Testimony of Job

"And the Lord restored Job's losses when he prayed for his friends. Indeed the Lord gave Job twice as much as he had before. Then all his brothers, all his sisters, and all those who had been his acquaintances before, came to him and ate food with him in his house; and they consoled him and comforted him for all the adversity that the Lord had brought upon him. Each one gave him a piece of silver and each a ring of gold. Now the Lord blessed the latter days of Job more than his beginning."

Job 42:10-12a

The Testimony of Ruth

"Then she fell on her face, bowed down to the ground, and said to him, 'why have I found favor in your eyes, that you should take notice of me, since I am a foreigner?' And Boaz answered and said to her, 'it has been fully reported to me, all that you have done for your mother-in-law since the death of your husband, and how you have left your father and mother and the land of your birth, and have now come to a people whom you did not know before. The Lord repay your work and a full reward be given you by the Lord God of Israel, under whose wings you have come for refuge.'"

Ruth 2:10-12

Chapter 8

DON'T DIE IN YOUR WILDERNESS

In light of all you have experienced, please allow me to give you a challenge. "Don't die in your wilderness." You have the ability to bounce back. Fight every battle. Learn every lesson. Get back in the race. Speak life! Encourage yourself. Embrace mobility. Do not settle. Hope for a brighter future. The Lord is on your side. He will never leave you. Your greatest days are ahead. Even though you may be in the darkest time of your life, hold your head up and continue walking. Each day is a day closer to you coming to the end of your wilderness experience.

Determined to Live

It is imperative that we understand that we can learn from other people's successes and mistakes. A life-long student will open his/her eyes to be enlightened from all angles. It has been estimated that there were over three million people that made the exit out of Egypt. Unfortunately, millions die in the wilderness due to disobedience, murmuring and complaining. In fact, God never intended the experience to take forty years. The Israelites changed what was supposed to be a great victory into tragic lost. None the less, I have great news! Your story can end differently. You can obtain the full promise God made concerning your life. Let me be honest, it will cost you. You must cultivate your determination in an effort to gain abundantly life. You will have to be relentless in dealing with challenges, tests and tragedy. You must search deep within and release your God-given passion. We can accept help from anybody, at anytime and anywhere. Just remember, it is impossible for a person to live your life for you. You have been trusted with your own wilderness experience. You will come out a better person. Yes, I said trusted! Deep within you is the ability to climb every mountain, survive every valley and be a testimony of the goodness of God. The Lord will do His part, but you must do yours.

"The Lord will fight for you, and you shall hold your peace. And the Lord said to Moses, 'why do you cry to me? Tell the children of Israel to go forward.'"

Exodus 14:14, 15

Did you notice the response of the Lord? First, He made it clear that He was there and would fight for them. Secondly, He said, "Why are you crying?" Crying is an expression of emotions. Be careful that you are not lead by your emotions in tough times. Making decisions based on emotions can cost you everything. He proceeds in giving Moses a profound command. "Go forward!"

Great Miracles Happen Under Great Pressure

"And the Angel of God, who went before the camp of Israel, moved and went behind them; and the pillar of cloud went from before them and stood behind them. So it came between the camp of the Egyptians and the camp of Israel. Thus it was a cloud

and darkness to the one, and it gave light by night to the other, so that the one did not come near the other all that night."

Exodus 14:19, 20

Wow! What an enormous display of the miraculous power of God! I just loved how the Angel of God moved from leading in the front, to covering them in the back. The reason God instructed them to "go forward," was because He had their back! Don't worry about what's behind you; God's got your back!

It would be unfair at the least, to say they should not have been concerned with having an enemy behind them. I'm certain they felt pressure. Perhaps this is how you feel right about now. Keep going forward my friend. There's a new day on the horizon. Do not be intimidated by fear. In my observation, I've personally found that the greatest times of need are opportunities for the greatest miracles. Many times the Lord will allow circumstances to arise to show His wondrous works. When He fixes it, there is no doubt that it was the mighty works of our God. Great miracles can happen under great pressure. In fact when you are experiencing your greatest test, it is an indication that the Lord is about to move with a mighty hand.

The Dawning of a New Day

"A new day is coming." "A new day is coming." Can you see it? Can you feel it? I know I have spoken of dreams, visions and the like. No, I am not a fanatic but I do realize the different ways the Lord speaks to me. At the beginning of this great wilderness experience I had another dream. In my dream I was in a huge building, with many different rooms. What seemed odd was that I was alone and everything in the building was of a grayish color. It was very dull and unattractive. My main objective was to find an exit. Oh, how I remember so clearly. I went from room to room in an effort to get out of this building. "I've got to get out of here. It is so unwelcoming. I've never been here before." These were just a few of my feelings and thoughts. Then it happened! After many attempts I walked out of this building and began to walk down the street. Wait! I have to tell you. As I proceeded to walk out I saw sunlight so bright, it could almost blind a person. Everything was bright, sunny, colorful and alive! It wasn't long before I figured out the interpretation. The big building represented my wilderness and what I was walking through. The diversity of rooms represented the different tests I would go through. The grayish color had to do with the trials and uncertainty. I walked out of those horrible tests into something filled with sunlight that is unexplainable. "It was the new day!" Can you see it? There were major blessings awaiting me. The blessings are not limited to only me and other clergy. God has a new day for you. All you have to do is; "Don't die in the wilderness."

The Bounce Back!

I must be totally honest and transparent. At the beginning of this wilderness experience, I was confused, disappointed and enormously afraid. I didn't know how my life would turn out. I was suffering silently, and wounded publicly. I just couldn't understand why the God I had served didn't prevent it. If that wasn't enough, every Sunday and Wednesday I had to stand in front of River of Life Church and speak life. I was given a charge to speak from a pure heart and to never allow venom, hatred, revenge or bitterness to take root within me. I am not suicidal and have never entertained the thoughts, but I had wished many days that the Lord would've taken me. After all, I was ready to go. I am enormously grateful that the Lord overlooked my pain and saw the road ahead.

Today I am alive! I am happy! I am continuously being restored. My greatest days are ahead and not behind. What I didn't know was that I was making a comeback each day. Little by little, I was bouncing back. Things were beginning to reform, renew, reshape and reinvent. I can honestly say that I am in the midst of my "bounce back." It is my prayer that you would strive for yours as well.

The Finale

One of the greatest and most important parts of a theatrical play is the last scene, "the finale." The finale is filled with excitement and the best acting and singing. The finale will almost always leave a long-lasting impression on the audience. I believe you can live life as God intended; with joy, peace, wholeness and love. How will your story end? What will your finale be? Just remember, in order to receive it, "Don't Die in Your Wilderness."

"The end of a thing is better than its beginning."

Ecclesiastes 7:8a

Bounce Back From Life Changing Events

RESOURCES

Merriam Webster Dictionary, 2004

New King James Version Bible, 1986

W.E. Vine, *Complete Expository Dictionary*, 1996

Bounce Back From Life Changing Events